With Fondest Memories of:

HONORING

Ms. Bee

The Hardest Part of Losing Someone,

Isn't Having to Say Goodbye, but

Rather Learning to **Live Without Them**.

Always Trying to Fill the Void, the Emptiness

That's Left Inside Your Heart When They Go.

~myowneulogy.com

If I'm having a tough day, my support system includes the following:

My therapist or mental health provider: _______________________________

____

____

My clergy: ____

____

My spouse/significant other: _______________________________________

____

Others I can rely on for support include: ________________________________

____

____

____

____

____

____

____

____

____

____

____

What I've learned about myself since living without you…

A thousand moments I had taken for granted, mostly because I assumed there would be a thousand more.

~Morgan Matson

HONORING
Ms. Bee

I remember this the most about you...

____

____

____

____

____

____

____

____

____

____

____

____

____

____

____

Sometimes all you can do is lie in bed and hope to fall asleep before you fall apart.

~William C. Hannan

HONORING
Ms. Bee

If you were here, I'd tell you...

Goodbyes are not forever. Goodbyes are not the end.
They simply mean I'll miss you until we meet again.

~Unknown

HONORING
Ms. Bee

This is what hurts me the most while living without you...

____

____

____

____

____

____

____

____

____

____

____

____

____

____

____

____

*May there be comfort in knowing someone so special
will never be forgotten.*

~Julie Hebert

30 Things I Can Do To Feel Better

Use this space to create a list of up to 30 activities you can engage in to feel better.

1. ______________________
2. ______________________
3. ______________________
4. ______________________
5. ______________________
6. ______________________
7. ______________________
8. ______________________
9. ______________________
10. ______________________
11. ______________________
12. ______________________
13. ______________________
14. ______________________
15. ______________________

16. ______________________
17. ______________________
18. ______________________
19. ______________________
20. ______________________
21. ______________________
22. ______________________
23. ______________________
24. ______________________
25. ______________________
26. ______________________
27. ______________________
28. ______________________
29. ______________________
30. ______________________

Date: /   /

If I need emotional support today, I will call:

____

My plans for today are: _______________________

____

____

My first thoughts of today: ___________________

____

My employer can help me during this time by:

____

I could use this from my spouse/significant other: ______________

____

I'm really missing this about you... ____________________________

____

Sometimes it feels like everyone has moved on, and I'm the only one that remembers you; that makes me...

____

____

I smiled when I remembered this about you... ____________________

____

____

I find it helpful when: ____

____

I am comforted by: ____

____

I feel your presence most when... _______________________________

____

If I can describe my day in one word, that word is: _____________

Today I:

☐ Feel supported
☐ Feel brokenhearted
☐ Feel misunderstood
☐ Feel angry
☐ Feel like crying
☐ Feel lonely
☐ Feel tired
☐ Feel sad
☐ Feel neutral
☐ Am taking it minute by minute

Date: ___ / ___ / ___

If I need emotional support today, I will call:

____

My plans for today are: ____________________________________

____

____

My first thoughts of today: ________________________________

____

My employer can help me during this time by:

____

I could use this from my spouse/significant other: _______________________________________

____

I'm really missing this about you... _______________________________________

____

Sometimes it feels like everyone has moved on, and I'm the only one that remembers you; that makes me...

____

____

I smiled when I remembered this about you... _______________________________________

____

____

I find it helpful when: _______________________________________

____

I am comforted by: _______________________________________

____

I feel your presence most when... _______________________________________

____

If I can describe my day in one word, that word is: _______________________________________

$\mathcal{D}$ate: /   /

If I need emotional support today, I will call:

____

My plans for today are: ___________________________

____

____

My first thoughts of today: _________________________

____

My employer can help me during this time by:

____

I could use this from my spouse/significant other: ___________________________

____

I'm really missing this about you... ___________________________________

____

Sometimes it feels like everyone has moved on, and I'm the only one that remembers you; that makes me...

____

____

I smiled when I remembered this about you... _____________________________

____

____

I find it helpful when: ____

____

I am comforted by: ____

____

I feel your presence most when... _____________________________________

____

If I can describe my day in one word, that word is: _______________________

Today I:

☐ Feel supported
☐ Feel brokenhearted
☐ Feel misunderstood
☐ Feel angry
☐ Feel like crying
☐ Feel lonely
☐ Feel tired
☐ Feel sad
☐ Feel neutral
☐ Am taking it minute by minute

Date: _____ / _____ / _____

<table>
<tr><td>

If I need emotional support today, I will call:

____

My plans for today are: _______________________

____

____

My first thoughts of today: ___________________

____

My employer can help me during this time by:

</td><td>

Today I:

☐ Feel supported

☐ Feel brokenhearted

☐ Feel misunderstood

☐ Feel angry

☐ Feel like crying

☐ Feel lonely

☐ Feel tired

☐ Feel sad

☐ Feel neutral

☐ Am taking it minute by minute

</td></tr>
</table>

____

I could use this from my spouse/significant other: ____________________

____

I'm really missing this about you... __________________________________

____

Sometimes it feels like everyone has moved on, and I'm the only one that remembers you; that makes me...

____

____

I smiled when I remembered this about you... __________________________

____

____

I find it helpful when: ____

____

I am comforted by: ____

____

I feel your presence most when... _____________________________________

____

If I can describe my day in one word, that word is: ___________________

Date: / /

If I need emotional support today, I will call:

____

My plans for today are: _________________________________

____

____

My first thoughts of today: ______________________________

____

My employer can help me during this time by:

____

I could use this from my spouse/significant other: ____________________________________

____

I'm really missing this about you... ____

____

Sometimes it feels like everyone has moved on, and I'm the only one that remembers you; that makes me...

____

____

I smiled when I remembered this about you... ____

____

____

I find it helpful when: ____

____

I am comforted by: ____

____

I feel your presence most when... ____

____

If I can describe my day in one word, that word is: _____________________________________

$\mathcal{D}ate$:   /   /

If I need emotional support today, I will call:

____ __________

My plans for today are: ____________________________________

____

____

My first thoughts of today: ________________________________

____

My employer can help me during this time by:

____

I could use this from my spouse/significant other: ___________________________

____

I'm really missing this about you... ____

____

Sometimes it feels like everyone has moved on, and I'm the only one that remembers you; that makes me...

____

____

I smiled when I remembered this about you... _________________________________

____

____

I find it helpful when: ____

____

I am comforted by: ____

____

I feel your presence most when... ____

____

If I can describe my day in one word, that word is: __________________________

<table>
<tr><td>Today I:</td></tr>
<tr><td>☐ Feel supported</td></tr>
<tr><td>☐ Feel brokenhearted</td></tr>
<tr><td>☐ Feel misunderstood</td></tr>
<tr><td>☐ Feel angry</td></tr>
<tr><td>☐ Feel like crying</td></tr>
<tr><td>☐ Feel lonely</td></tr>
<tr><td>☐ Feel tired</td></tr>
<tr><td>☐ Feel sad</td></tr>
<tr><td>☐ Feel neutral</td></tr>
<tr><td>☐ Am taking it minute by minute</td></tr>
</table>

Date: /   /

If I need emotional support today, I will call:

____

My plans for today are: ______________________________

____

____

My first thoughts of today: ____________________________

____

My employer can help me during this time by:

____

I could use this from my spouse/significant other: ____________________________

____

I'm really missing this about you... ____________________________

____

Sometimes it feels like everyone has moved on, and I'm the only one that remembers you; that makes me...

____

____

I smiled when I remembered this about you... ____________________________

____

____

I find it helpful when: ____________________________

____

I am comforted by: ____________________________

____

I feel your presence most when... ____________________________

____

If I can describe my day in one word, that word is: ____________________________

<table>
<tr><td>Today I:</td></tr>
<tr><td>☐ Feel supported</td></tr>
<tr><td>☐ Feel brokenhearted</td></tr>
<tr><td>☐ Feel misunderstood</td></tr>
<tr><td>☐ Feel angry</td></tr>
<tr><td>☐ Feel like crying</td></tr>
<tr><td>☐ Feel lonely</td></tr>
<tr><td>☐ Feel tired</td></tr>
<tr><td>☐ Feel sad</td></tr>
<tr><td>☐ Feel neutral</td></tr>
<tr><td>☐ Am taking it minute by minute</td></tr>
</table>

Date: / /

If I need emotional support today, I will call:

____

My plans for today are: _______________________________

____

____

My first thoughts of today: _______________________________

____

My employer can help me during this time by:

____

I could use this from my spouse/significant other: _______________________________

____

I'm really missing this about you... _______________________________

____

Sometimes it feels like everyone has moved on, and I'm the only one that remembers you; that makes me...

____

____

I smiled when I remembered this about you... _______________________________

____

____

I find it helpful when: _______________________________

____

I am comforted by: _______________________________

____

I feel your presence most when... _______________________________

____

If I can describe my day in one word, that word is: _______________________________

Today I:

☐ Feel supported
☐ Feel brokenhearted
☐ Feel misunderstood
☐ Feel angry
☐ Feel like crying
☐ Feel lonely
☐ Feel tired
☐ Feel sad
☐ Feel neutral
☐ Am taking it minute by minute

$Date:$ ___ / ___ / ___

If I need emotional support today, I will call:

____

My plans for today are: _______________________

____

____

My first thoughts of today: ___________________

____

My employer can help me during this time by:

____

I could use this from my spouse/significant other: _______________________

____

I'm really missing this about you... _______________________

____

Sometimes it feels like everyone has moved on, and I'm the only one that remembers you; that makes me...

____

____

I smiled when I remembered this about you... _______________________

____

____

I find it helpful when: _______________________

____

I am comforted by: _______________________

____

I feel your presence most when... _______________________

____

If I can describe my day in one word, that word is: _______________________

Today I:

- ☐ Feel supported
- ☐ Feel brokenhearted
- ☐ Feel misunderstood
- ☐ Feel angry
- ☐ Feel like crying
- ☐ Feel lonely
- ☐ Feel tired
- ☐ Feel sad
- ☐ Feel neutral
- ☐ Am taking it minute by minute

Date: /   /

If I need emotional support today, I will call:

____

My plans for today are: ______________________________

____

____

My first thoughts of today: ______________________________

____

My employer can help me during this time by:

____

I could use this from my spouse/significant other: ______________________________

____

I'm really missing this about you... ______________________________

____

Sometimes it feels like everyone has moved on, and I'm the only one that remembers you; that makes me...

____

____

I smiled when I remembered this about you... ______________________________

____

____

I find it helpful when: ______________________________

____

I am comforted by: ______________________________

____

I feel your presence most when... ______________________________

____

If I can describe my day in one word, that word is: ______________________________

Date: /   /

If I need emotional support today, I will call:

____

My plans for today are: _________________________

____

____

My first thoughts of today: _____________________

____

My employer can help me during this time by:

____

I could use this from my spouse/significant other: _______________________

____

I'm really missing this about you... _______________________

____

Sometimes it feels like everyone has moved on, and I'm the only one that remembers you; that makes me...

____

____

I smiled when I remembered this about you... _______________________

____

____

I find it helpful when: _______________________

____

I am comforted by: _______________________

____

I feel your presence most when... _______________________

____

If I can describe my day in one word, that word is: _______________________

Today I:

☐ Feel supported

☐ Feel brokenhearted

☐ Feel misunderstood

☐ Feel angry

☐ Feel like crying

☐ Feel lonely

☐ Feel tired

☐ Feel sad

☐ Feel neutral

☐ Am taking it minute by minute

Date: ___ / ___ / ___

If I need emotional support today, I will call:

____

My plans for today are: _______________________________

____

____

My first thoughts of today: _______________________________

____

My employer can help me during this time by:

____

I could use this from my spouse/significant other: _______________________________

____

I'm really missing this about you... _______________________________

____

Sometimes it feels like everyone has moved on, and I'm the only one that remembers you; that makes me...

____

____

I smiled when I remembered this about you... _______________________________

____

____

I find it helpful when: _______________________________

____

I am comforted by: _______________________________

____

I feel your presence most when... _______________________________

____

If I can describe my day in one word, that word is: _______________________________

$\mathcal{D}ate$:   /   /

If I need emotional support today, I will call:

____

My plans for today are: ______________________________

____

____

My first thoughts of today: ___________________________

____

My employer can help me during this time by:

____

I could use this from my spouse/significant other: ___________________________

____

I'm really missing this about you... ___________________________

____

Sometimes it feels like everyone has moved on, and I'm the only one that remembers you; that makes me...

____

____

I smiled when I remembered this about you... ___________________________

____

____

I find it helpful when: ___________________________

____

I am comforted by: ___________________________

____

I feel your presence most when... ___________________________

____

If I can describe my day in one word, that word is: ___________________________

Today I:
- ☐ Feel supported
- ☐ Feel brokenhearted
- ☐ Feel misunderstood
- ☐ Feel angry
- ☐ Feel like crying
- ☐ Feel lonely
- ☐ Feel tired
- ☐ Feel sad
- ☐ Feel neutral
- ☐ Am taking it minute by minute

Date: ___ / ___ / ___

If I need emotional support today, I will call:

____

My plans for today are: _______________________

____

____

My first thoughts of today: ___________________

____

My employer can help me during this time by:

____

I could use this from my spouse/significant other: _______________________

____

I'm really missing this about you... ___________

____

Sometimes it feels like everyone has moved on, and I'm the only one that remembers you; that makes me...

____

____

I smiled when I remembered this about you... ___

____

____

I find it helpful when: ________________________

____

I am comforted by: _____________________________

____

I feel your presence most when... ______________

____

If I can describe my day in one word, that word is: _______________

Today I:
- ☐ Feel supported
- ☐ Feel brokenhearted
- ☐ Feel misunderstood
- ☐ Feel angry
- ☐ Feel like crying
- ☐ Feel lonely
- ☐ Feel tired
- ☐ Feel sad
- ☐ Feel neutral
- ☐ Am taking it minute by minute

Date: /   /

If I need emotional support today, I will call:

____

My plans for today are: _______________________

____

____

My first thoughts of today: ___________________

____

My employer can help me during this time by:

____

I could use this from my spouse/significant other: _______________________

____

I'm really missing this about you... _______________________

____

Sometimes it feels like everyone has moved on, and I'm the only one that remembers you; that makes me...

____

____

I smiled when I remembered this about you... _______________________

____

____

I find it helpful when: _______________________

____

I am comforted by: _______________________

____

I feel your presence most when... _______________________

____

If I can describe my day in one word, that word is: _______________________

Today I:

☐ Feel supported
☐ Feel brokenhearted
☐ Feel misunderstood
☐ Feel angry
☐ Feel like crying
☐ Feel lonely
☐ Feel tired
☐ Feel sad
☐ Feel neutral
☐ Am taking it minute by minute

Date: ___ / ___ / ___

If I need emotional support today, I will call:

____

My plans for today are: _______________________

____

____

My first thoughts of today: ___________________

____

My employer can help me during this time by:

____

I could use this from my spouse/significant other: _______________________

____

I'm really missing this about you... _______________________

____

Sometimes it feels like everyone has moved on, and I'm the only one that remembers you; that makes me...

____

____

I smiled when I remembered this about you... _______________________

____

____

I find it helpful when: _______________________

____

I am comforted by: _______________________

____

I feel your presence most when... _______________________

____

If I can describe my day in one word, that word is: _______________________

Today I:

☐ Feel supported
☐ Feel brokenhearted
☐ Feel misunderstood
☐ Feel angry
☐ Feel like crying
☐ Feel lonely
☐ Feel tired
☐ Feel sad
☐ Feel neutral
☐ Am taking it minute by minute

Date: / /

If I need emotional support today, I will call:

____

My plans for today are: _______________________

____

____

My first thoughts of today: ____________________

____

My employer can help me during this time by:

____

I could use this from my spouse/significant other: _______________________

____

I'm really missing this about you... _______________________

____

Sometimes it feels like everyone has moved on, and I'm the only one that remembers you; that makes me...

____

____

I smiled when I remembered this about you... _______________________

____

____

I find it helpful when: _______________________

____

I am comforted by: _______________________

____

I feel your presence most when... _______________________

____

If I can describe my day in one word, that word is: _______________________

Date: ___ / ___ / ___

If I need emotional support today, I will call:

____

My plans for today are: _______________________

____

____

My first thoughts of today: ___________________

____

My employer can help me during this time by:

____

I could use this from my spouse/significant other: _______________

____

I'm really missing this about you... _______________________

____

Sometimes it feels like everyone has moved on, and I'm the only one that remembers you; that makes me...

____

____

I smiled when I remembered this about you... _______________

____

____

I find it helpful when: _____________________________

____

I am comforted by: _________________________________

____

I feel your presence most when... __________________________

____

If I can describe my day in one word, that word is: _______________

Date: / /

If I need emotional support today, I will call:

____

My plans for today are: _______________________

____

____

My first thoughts of today: ___________________

____

My employer can help me during this time by:

____

I could use this from my spouse/significant other: _______________________

____

I'm really missing this about you... _____________________________________

____

Sometimes it feels like everyone has moved on, and I'm the only one that remembers you; that makes me...

____

____

I smiled when I remembered this about you... ____________________________

____

____

I find it helpful when: ____

____

I am comforted by: ____

____

I feel your presence most when... ____

____

If I can describe my day in one word, that word is: ______________________

Date: /   /

If I need emotional support today, I will call:

____

My plans for today are: _________________________________

____

____

My first thoughts of today: ______________________________

____

My employer can help me during this time by:

____

I could use this from my spouse/significant other: _____________________________

____

I'm really missing this about you... ____

____

Sometimes it feels like everyone has moved on, and I'm the only one that remembers
you; that makes me...

____

____

I smiled when I remembered this about you... ___________________________________

____

____

I find it helpful when: ____

____

I am comforted by: ____

____

I feel your presence most when... ____

____

If I can describe my day in one word, that word is: ______________________________

Today I:

☐ Feel supported
☐ Feel brokenhearted
☐ Feel misunderstood
☐ Feel angry
☐ Feel like crying
☐ Feel lonely
☐ Feel tired
☐ Feel sad
☐ Feel neutral
☐ Am taking it minute by minute

Date: ___ / ___ / ___

<table>
<tr><td>

If I need emotional support today, I will call:

____

My plans for today are: _______________

____

____

My first thoughts of today: _____________

____

My employer can help me during this time by:

</td><td>

Today I:

☐ Feel supported
☐ Feel brokenhearted
☐ Feel misunderstood
☐ Feel angry
☐ Feel like crying
☐ Feel lonely
☐ Feel tired
☐ Feel sad
☐ Feel neutral
☐ Am taking it minute by minute

</td></tr>
</table>

____

I could use this from my spouse/significant other: _______________________

____

I'm really missing this about you... _______________________________

____

Sometimes it feels like everyone has moved on, and I'm the only one that remembers you; that makes me...

____

____

I smiled when I remembered this about you... ___________________________

____

____

I find it helpful when: ____

____

I am comforted by: ____

____

I feel your presence most when... ___________________________________

____

If I can describe my day in one word, that word is: ______________________

Date: ____ / ____ / ____

If I need emotional support today, I will call:

____

My plans for today are: _______________________

____

____

My first thoughts of today: ____________________

____

My employer can help me during this time by:

____

I could use this from my spouse/significant other: _______________________

____

I'm really missing this about you... _____________________________________

____

Sometimes it feels like everyone has moved on, and I'm the only one that remembers you; that makes me...

____

____

I smiled when I remembered this about you... ____________________________

____

____

I find it helpful when: ____

____

I am comforted by: ____

____

I feel your presence most when... _______________________________________

____

If I can describe my day in one word, that word is: ______________________

Date: /   /

If I need emotional support today, I will call:

____

My plans for today are: _______________________

____

____

My first thoughts of today: ___________________

____

My employer can help me during this time by:

____

I could use this from my spouse/significant other: ______________________

____

I'm really missing this about you... ____________________________________

____

Sometimes it feels like everyone has moved on, and I'm the only one that remembers you; that makes me...

____

____

I smiled when I remembered this about you... ____________________________

____

____

I find it helpful when: ____

____

I am comforted by: ____

____

I feel your presence most when... _______________________________________

____

If I can describe my day in one word, that word is: ______________________

Date: /   /

If I need emotional support today, I will call:

____

My plans for today are: _______________________

____

____

My first thoughts of today: ___________________

____

My employer can help me during this time by:

____

I could use this from my spouse/significant other: ______________________

____

I'm really missing this about you... ____________________________________

____

Sometimes it feels like everyone has moved on, and I'm the only one that remembers you; that makes me...

____

____

I smiled when I remembered this about you... ____________________________

____

____

I find it helpful when: ____

____

I am comforted by: ____

____

I feel your presence most when... _______________________________________

____

If I can describe my day in one word, that word is: _____________________

<table>
<tr><td>Today I:</td></tr>
<tr><td>☐ Feel supported</td></tr>
<tr><td>☐ Feel brokenhearted</td></tr>
<tr><td>☐ Feel misunderstood</td></tr>
<tr><td>☐ Feel angry</td></tr>
<tr><td>☐ Feel like crying</td></tr>
<tr><td>☐ Feel lonely</td></tr>
<tr><td>☐ Feel tired</td></tr>
<tr><td>☐ Feel sad</td></tr>
<tr><td>☐ Feel neutral</td></tr>
<tr><td>☐ Am taking it minute by minute</td></tr>
</table>

Date: / /

If I need emotional support today, I will call:

____

My plans for today are: _______________________

____

____

My first thoughts of today: ___________________

____

My employer can help me during this time by:

____

I could use this from my spouse/significant other: _______________________

____

I'm really missing this about you... _______________________

____

Sometimes it feels like everyone has moved on, and I'm the only one that remembers you; that makes me...

____

____

I smiled when I remembered this about you... _______________________

____

____

I find it helpful when: _______________________

____

I am comforted by: _______________________

____

I feel your presence most when... _______________________

____

If I can describe my day in one word, that word is: _______________________

Today I:

☐ Feel supported
☐ Feel brokenhearted
☐ Feel misunderstood
☐ Feel angry
☐ Feel like crying
☐ Feel lonely
☐ Feel tired
☐ Feel sad
☐ Feel neutral
☐ Am taking it minute by minute

$\mathcal{D}ate$:   /   /

If I need emotional support today, I will call:

____

My plans for today are: _________________________________

____

____

My first thoughts of today: _________________________________

____

My employer can help me during this time by:

____

I could use this from my spouse/significant other: _______________________________

____

I'm really missing this about you... _______________________________________

____

Sometimes it feels like everyone has moved on, and I'm the only one that remembers you; that makes me...

____

____

I smiled when I remembered this about you... _______________________________

____

____

I find it helpful when: ____

____

I am comforted by: ____

____

I feel your presence most when... _________________________________

____

If I can describe my day in one word, that word is: _______________________

Today I:

☐ Feel supported
☐ Feel brokenhearted
☐ Feel misunderstood
☐ Feel angry
☐ Feel like crying
☐ Feel lonely
☐ Feel tired
☐ Feel sad
☐ Feel neutral
☐ Am taking it minute by minute

Date: ___ / ___ / ___

If I need emotional support today, I will call:

____

My plans for today are: _______________________

____

____

My first thoughts of today: ___________________

____

My employer can help me during this time by:

____

I could use this from my spouse/significant other: _______________________

____

I'm really missing this about you... _______________________

____

Sometimes it feels like everyone has moved on, and I'm the only one that remembers you; that makes me...

____

____

I smiled when I remembered this about you... _______________________

____

____

I find it helpful when: _______________________

____

I am comforted by: _______________________

____

I feel your presence most when... _______________________

____

If I can describe my day in one word, that word is: _______________________

Date: / /

If I need emotional support today, I will call:

____

My plans for today are: _______________________________

____

____

My first thoughts of today: _____________________________

____

My employer can help me during this time by:

____

I could use this from my spouse/significant other: _______________________________

____

I'm really missing this about you... _______________________________

____

Sometimes it feels like everyone has moved on, and I'm the only one that remembers you; that makes me...

____

____

I smiled when I remembered this about you... _______________________________

____

I find it helpful when: _______________________________

____

I am comforted by: _______________________________

____

I feel your presence most when... _______________________________

____

If I can describe my day in one word, that word is: _______________________________

Today I:

☐ Feel supported
☐ Feel brokenhearted
☐ Feel misunderstood
☐ Feel angry
☐ Feel like crying
☐ Feel lonely
☐ Feel tired
☐ Feel sad
☐ Feel neutral
☐ Am taking it minute by minute

Date: /   /

If I need emotional support today, I will call:

____

My plans for today are: _______________________________

____

____

My first thoughts of today: _______________________________

____

My employer can help me during this time by:

____

I could use this from my spouse/significant other: _______________________________

____

I'm really missing this about you... _______________________________

____

Sometimes it feels like everyone has moved on, and I'm the only one that remembers you; that makes me...

____

____

I smiled when I remembered this about you... _______________________________

____

____

I find it helpful when: _______________________________

____

I am comforted by: _______________________________

____

I feel your presence most when... _______________________________

____

If I can describe my day in one word, that word is: _______________________________

Date: /   /

If I need emotional support today, I will call:

____

My plans for today are: _______________________

____

____

My first thoughts of today: ____________________

____

My employer can help me during this time by:

____

I could use this from my spouse/significant other: _______________________________

____

I'm really missing this about you... ____

____

Sometimes it feels like everyone has moved on, and I'm the only one that remembers you; that makes me...

____

____

I smiled when I remembered this about you... _______________________________

____

____

I find it helpful when: _______________________________

____

I am comforted by: _______________________________

____

I feel your presence most when... _______________________________

____

If I can describe my day in one word, that word is: _______________________

Today I:

☐ Feel supported
☐ Feel brokenhearted
☐ Feel misunderstood
☐ Feel angry
☐ Feel like crying
☐ Feel lonely
☐ Feel tired
☐ Feel sad
☐ Feel neutral
☐ Am taking it minute by minute

$\mathcal{D}ate$:   /   /

If I need emotional support today, I will call:

____

My plans for today are: ______________________________

____

____

My first thoughts of today: __________________________

____

My employer can help me during this time by:

____

I could use this from my spouse/significant other: _______________________________

____

I'm really missing this about you... ____

____

Sometimes it feels like everyone has moved on, and I'm the only one that remembers you; that makes me...

____

____

I smiled when I remembered this about you... _______________________________

____

____

I find it helpful when: ____

____

I am comforted by: ____

____

I feel your presence most when... ____

____

If I can describe my day in one word, that word is: _______________________________

Date: /   /

If I need emotional support today, I will call:

____

My plans for today are: _______________________

____

____

My first thoughts of today: ___________________

____

My employer can help me during this time by:

____

I could use this from my spouse/significant other: _______________________________

____

I'm really missing this about you... _______________________________________

____

Sometimes it feels like everyone has moved on, and I'm the only one that remembers you; that makes me...

____

____

I smiled when I remembered this about you... _______________________________

____

____

I find it helpful when: ____

____

I am comforted by: ____

____

I feel your presence most when... _______________________________________

____

If I can describe my day in one word, that word is: _______________________

Today I:

☐ Feel supported
☐ Feel brokenhearted
☐ Feel misunderstood
☐ Feel angry
☐ Feel like crying
☐ Feel lonely
☐ Feel tired
☐ Feel sad
☐ Feel neutral
☐ Am taking it minute by minute

Date: / /

If I need emotional support today, I will call:

____

My plans for today are: ______________________________

____

____

My first thoughts of today: ______________________________

____

My employer can help me during this time by:

____

I could use this from my spouse/significant other: ______________________________

____

I'm really missing this about you... ______________________________

____

Sometimes it feels like everyone has moved on, and I'm the only one that remembers you; that makes me...

____

____

I smiled when I remembered this about you... ______________________________

____

____

I find it helpful when: ______________________________

____

I am comforted by: ______________________________

____

I feel your presence most when... ______________________________

____

If I can describe my day in one word, that word is: ______________________________

Date: /   /

If I need emotional support today, I will call:

____

My plans for today are: ______________________________

____

____

My first thoughts of today: __________________________

____

My employer can help me during this time by:

____

I could use this from my spouse/significant other: _______________________________

____

I'm really missing this about you... _______________________________________

____

Sometimes it feels like everyone has moved on, and I'm the only one that remembers
you; that makes me...

____

____

I smiled when I remembered this about you... ____________________________________

____

____

I find it helpful when: ____

____

I am comforted by: ____

____

I feel your presence most when... ____

____

If I can describe my day in one word, that word is: ______________________________

Date: /   /

If I need emotional support today, I will call:

____

My plans for today are: _______________________

____

____

My first thoughts of today: ___________________

____

My employer can help me during this time by:

____

I could use this from my spouse/significant other: _______________________

____

I'm really missing this about you... _______________________

____

Sometimes it feels like everyone has moved on, and I'm the only one that remembers you; that makes me...

____

____

I smiled when I remembered this about you... _______________________

____

____

I find it helpful when: _______________________

____

I am comforted by: _______________________

____

I feel your presence most when... _______________________

____

If I can describe my day in one word, that word is: _______________________

Date: ___ / ___ / ___

If I need emotional support today, I will call:

____

My plans for today are: _______________________

____

____

My first thoughts of today: ___________________

____

My employer can help me during this time by:

____

I could use this from my spouse/significant other: _______________________

____

I'm really missing this about you... ______________________________

____

Sometimes it feels like everyone has moved on, and I'm the only one that remembers you; that makes me...

____

____

I smiled when I remembered this about you... _____________________

____

____

I find it helpful when: ____

____

I am comforted by: ____

____

I feel your presence most when... ________________________________

____

If I can describe my day in one word, that word is: ______________

Today I:

☐ Feel supported
☐ Feel brokenhearted
☐ Feel misunderstood
☐ Feel angry
☐ Feel like crying
☐ Feel lonely
☐ Feel tired
☐ Feel sad
☐ Feel neutral
☐ Am taking it minute by minute

Date: /   /

If I need emotional support today, I will call:

____

My plans for today are: _________________________________

____

____

My first thoughts of today: ______________________________

____

My employer can help me during this time by:

____

I could use this from my spouse/significant other: ___________________________

____

I'm really missing this about you... ___________________________________

____

Sometimes it feels like everyone has moved on, and I'm the only one that remembers you; that makes me...

____

____

I smiled when I remembered this about you... _______________________________

____

____

I find it helpful when: ____

____

I am comforted by: ____

____

I feel your presence most when... ___________________________________

____

If I can describe my day in one word, that word is: _________________________

Today I:

- ☐ Feel supported
- ☐ Feel brokenhearted
- ☐ Feel misunderstood
- ☐ Feel angry
- ☐ Feel like crying
- ☐ Feel lonely
- ☐ Feel tired
- ☐ Feel sad
- ☐ Feel neutral
- ☐ Am taking it minute by minute

Date: ___/___/___

If I need emotional support today, I will call:

____

My plans for today are: _______________________

____

____

My first thoughts of today: ____________________

____

My employer can help me during this time by:

____

I could use this from my spouse/significant other: ____

____

I'm really missing this about you... ____

____

Sometimes it feels like everyone has moved on, and I'm the only one that remembers you; that makes me...

____

____

I smiled when I remembered this about you... ____

____

____

I find it helpful when: ____

____

I am comforted by: ____

____

I feel your presence most when... ____

____

If I can describe my day in one word, that word is: ____

Today I:

☐ Feel supported
☐ Feel brokenhearted
☐ Feel misunderstood
☐ Feel angry
☐ Feel like crying
☐ Feel lonely
☐ Feel tired
☐ Feel sad
☐ Feel neutral
☐ Am taking it minute by minute

Date: /   /

If I need emotional support today, I will call:

____

My plans for today are: _______________________

____

____

My first thoughts of today: ____________________

____

My employer can help me during this time by:

____

I could use this from my spouse/significant other: _______________________

____

I'm really missing this about you... ____________________________________

____

Sometimes it feels like everyone has moved on, and I'm the only one that remembers you; that makes me...

____

____

I smiled when I remembered this about you... ____________________________

____

____

I find it helpful when: ____

____

I am comforted by: ____

____

I feel your presence most when... _______________________________________

____

If I can describe my day in one word, that word is: ______________________

Today I:

☐ Feel supported
☐ Feel brokenhearted
☐ Feel misunderstood
☐ Feel angry
☐ Feel like crying
☐ Feel lonely
☐ Feel tired
☐ Feel sad
☐ Feel neutral
☐ Am taking it minute by minute

$\mathcal{Date}$:   /   /

If I need emotional support today, I will call:

____

My plans for today are: _______________________

____

____

My first thoughts of today: ____________________

____

My employer can help me during this time by:

____

I could use this from my spouse/significant other: _______________________

____

I'm really missing this about you... _______________________________

____

Sometimes it feels like everyone has moved on, and I'm the only one that remembers you; that makes me...

____

____

I smiled when I remembered this about you... __________________________

____

____

I find it helpful when: ____

____

I am comforted by: ____

____

I feel your presence most when... ____________________________________

____

If I can describe my day in one word, that word is: ____________________

Today I:

- ☐ Feel supported
- ☐ Feel brokenhearted
- ☐ Feel misunderstood
- ☐ Feel angry
- ☐ Feel like crying
- ☐ Feel lonely
- ☐ Feel tired
- ☐ Feel sad
- ☐ Feel neutral
- ☐ Am taking it minute by minute

Date: / /

If I need emotional support today, I will call:

____

My plans for today are: ______________________

____

____

My first thoughts of today: __________________

____

My employer can help me during this time by:

____

I could use this from my spouse/significant other: _______________________

____

I'm really missing this about you... ___________________________

____

Sometimes it feels like everyone has moved on, and I'm the only one that remembers you; that makes me...

____

____

I smiled when I remembered this about you... _______________________

____

____

I find it helpful when: _______________________

____

I am comforted by: ___________________________

____

I feel your presence most when... _____________________

____

If I can describe my day in one word, that word is: _______________________

Today I:

☐ Feel supported
☐ Feel brokenhearted
☐ Feel misunderstood
☐ Feel angry
☐ Feel like crying
☐ Feel lonely
☐ Feel tired
☐ Feel sad
☐ Feel neutral
☐ Am taking it minute by minute

Date: /   /

If I need emotional support today, I will call:

____

My plans for today are: _______________________

____

____

My first thoughts of today: ____________________

____

My employer can help me during this time by:

____

I could use this from my spouse/significant other: ____

____

I'm really missing this about you... ____

____

Sometimes it feels like everyone has moved on, and I'm the only one that remembers you; that makes me...

____

____

I smiled when I remembered this about you... ____

____

____

I find it helpful when: ____

____

I am comforted by: ____

____

I feel your presence most when... ____

____

If I can describe my day in one word, that word is: _______________________________________

Today I:

- ☐ Feel supported
- ☐ Feel brokenhearted
- ☐ Feel misunderstood
- ☐ Feel angry
- ☐ Feel like crying
- ☐ Feel lonely
- ☐ Feel tired
- ☐ Feel sad
- ☐ Feel neutral
- ☐ Am taking it minute by minute

$\mathcal{D}$ate: ___ / ___ / ___

If I need emotional support today, I will call:

____

My plans for today are: _______________________

____

____

My first thoughts of today: ___________________

____

My employer can help me during this time by:

____

I could use this from my spouse/significant other: ______________________

____

I'm really missing this about you... ____________________________________

____

Sometimes it feels like everyone has moved on, and I'm the only one that remembers you; that makes me...

____

____

I smiled when I remembered this about you... ___________________________

____

____

I find it helpful when: ____

____

I am comforted by: ____

____

I feel your presence most when... ______________________________________

____

If I can describe my day in one word, that word is: ____________________

Today I:

☐ Feel supported

☐ Feel brokenhearted

☐ Feel misunderstood

☐ Feel angry

☐ Feel like crying

☐ Feel lonely

☐ Feel tired

☐ Feel sad

☐ Feel neutral

☐ Am taking it minute by minute

Date: /   /

If I need emotional support today, I will call:

____

My plans for today are: _________________________

____

____

My first thoughts of today: ______________________

____

My employer can help me during this time by:

____

I could use this from my spouse/significant other: ________________________________

____

I'm really missing this about you... _______________________________________

____

Sometimes it feels like everyone has moved on, and I'm the only one that remembers you; that makes me...

____

____

I smiled when I remembered this about you... _______________________________

____

____

I find it helpful when: ____

____

I am comforted by: ____

____

I feel your presence most when... ____

____

If I can describe my day in one word, that word is: ________________________

<table>
<tr><td>Today I:</td></tr>
<tr><td>☐ Feel supported</td></tr>
<tr><td>☐ Feel brokenhearted</td></tr>
<tr><td>☐ Feel misunderstood</td></tr>
<tr><td>☐ Feel angry</td></tr>
<tr><td>☐ Feel like crying</td></tr>
<tr><td>☐ Feel lonely</td></tr>
<tr><td>☐ Feel tired</td></tr>
<tr><td>☐ Feel sad</td></tr>
<tr><td>☐ Feel neutral</td></tr>
<tr><td>☐ Am taking it minute by minute</td></tr>
</table>

Date: / /

If I need emotional support today, I will call:

____

My plans for today are: _________________________

____

____

My first thoughts of today: _____________________

____

My employer can help me during this time by:

____

I could use this from my spouse/significant other: _____________________

____

I'm really missing this about you... _____________________

____

Sometimes it feels like everyone has moved on, and I'm the only one that remembers you; that makes me...

____

____

I smiled when I remembered this about you... _____________________

____

____

I find it helpful when: _____________________

____

I am comforted by: _____________________

____

I feel your presence most when... _____________________

____

If I can describe my day in one word, that word is: _____________________

Today I:

- ☐ Feel supported
- ☐ Feel brokenhearted
- ☐ Feel misunderstood
- ☐ Feel angry
- ☐ Feel like crying
- ☐ Feel lonely
- ☐ Feel tired
- ☐ Feel sad
- ☐ Feel neutral
- ☐ Am taking it minute by minute

$Date$:   /   /

If I need emotional support today, I will call:

____

My plans for today are: _______________________________

____

____

My first thoughts of today: _______________________

____

My employer can help me during this time by:

____

I could use this from my spouse/significant other: _______________________________________

____

I'm really missing this about you... _______________________________________

____

Sometimes it feels like everyone has moved on, and I'm the only one that remembers you; that makes me...

____

____

I smiled when I remembered this about you... _______________________________________

____

____

I find it helpful when: _______________________________________

____

I am comforted by: _______________________________________

____

I feel your presence most when... _______________________________________

____

If I can describe my day in one word, that word is: _______________________

Today I:

☐ Feel supported
☐ Feel brokenhearted
☐ Feel misunderstood
☐ Feel angry
☐ Feel like crying
☐ Feel lonely
☐ Feel tired
☐ Feel sad
☐ Feel neutral
☐ Am taking it minute by minute

Date: / /

If I need emotional support today, I will call:

____

My plans for today are: ____________________

____

____

My first thoughts of today: ________________

____

My employer can help me during this time by:

____

I could use this from my spouse/significant other: _______________

____

I'm really missing this about you... _______________

____

Sometimes it feels like everyone has moved on, and I'm the only one that remembers you; that makes me...

____

____

I smiled when I remembered this about you... _______________

____

____

I find it helpful when: _______________

____

I am comforted by: _______________

____

I feel your presence most when... _______________

____

If I can describe my day in one word, that word is: _______________

Today I:

☐ Feel supported
☐ Feel brokenhearted
☐ Feel misunderstood
☐ Feel angry
☐ Feel like crying
☐ Feel lonely
☐ Feel tired
☐ Feel sad
☐ Feel neutral
☐ Am taking it minute by minute

Date: / /

If I need emotional support today, I will call:

____

My plans for today are: ____________________________

____

____

My first thoughts of today: _________________________

____

My employer can help me during this time by:

____

I could use this from my spouse/significant other: ____________________________

____

I'm really missing this about you... ____________________________

____

Sometimes it feels like everyone has moved on, and I'm the only one that remembers you; that makes me...

____

____

I smiled when I remembered this about you... ____________________________

____

____

I find it helpful when: ____________________________

____

I am comforted by: ____________________________

____

I feel your presence most when... ____________________________

____

If I can describe my day in one word, that word is: ____________________________

Date: /   /

If I need emotional support today, I will call:

____

My plans for today are: _______________________

____

____

My first thoughts of today: ____________________

____

My employer can help me during this time by:

<table>
<tr><td>Today I:</td></tr>
<tr><td>☐ Feel supported</td></tr>
<tr><td>☐ Feel brokenhearted</td></tr>
<tr><td>☐ Feel misunderstood</td></tr>
<tr><td>☐ Feel angry</td></tr>
<tr><td>☐ Feel like crying</td></tr>
<tr><td>☐ Feel lonely</td></tr>
<tr><td>☐ Feel tired</td></tr>
<tr><td>☐ Feel sad</td></tr>
<tr><td>☐ Feel neutral</td></tr>
<tr><td>☐ Am taking it minute by minute</td></tr>
</table>

____

I could use this from my spouse/significant other: ______________________

____

I'm really missing this about you... ______________________________

____

Sometimes it feels like everyone has moved on, and I'm the only one that remembers you; that makes me...

____

____

I smiled when I remembered this about you... _______________________

____

____

I find it helpful when: _________________________

____

I am comforted by: ____________________________

____

I feel your presence most when... _______________________

____

If I can describe my day in one word, that word is: ______________________

Date: /   /

If I need emotional support today, I will call:

____

My plans for today are: _________________________

____

____

My first thoughts of today: ______________________

____

My employer can help me during this time by:

____

I could use this from my spouse/significant other: _______________________________

____

I'm really missing this about you... ____

____

Sometimes it feels like everyone has moved on, and I'm the only one that remembers you; that makes me...

____

____

I smiled when I remembered this about you... ____________________________________

____

____

I find it helpful when: ____

____

I am comforted by: ____

____

I feel your presence most when... ____

____

If I can describe my day in one word, that word is: _______________________________

Date: /   /

If I need emotional support today, I will call:

____

My plans for today are: _______________________

____

____

My first thoughts of today: ____________________

____

My employer can help me during this time by:

____

I could use this from my spouse/significant other: _______________________

____

I'm really missing this about you... _____________

____

Sometimes it feels like everyone has moved on, and I'm the only one that remembers you; that makes me...

____

____

I smiled when I remembered this about you... _____________

____

____

I find it helpful when: _________________________

____

I am comforted by: ___________________________

____

I feel your presence most when... _______________

____

If I can describe my day in one word, that word is: _______________

Date: /   /

If I need emotional support today, I will call:

____

My plans for today are: _______________________

____

____

My first thoughts of today: ____________________

____

My employer can help me during this time by:

____

I could use this from my spouse/significant other: _______________________________

____

I'm really missing this about you... _______________________________

____

Sometimes it feels like everyone has moved on, and I'm the only one that remembers you; that makes me...

____

____

I smiled when I remembered this about you... _______________________________

____

____

I find it helpful when: _______________________________

____

I am comforted by: _______________________________

____

I feel your presence most when... _______________________________

____

If I can describe my day in one word, that word is: _______________________________

Today I:

☐ Feel supported
☐ Feel brokenhearted
☐ Feel misunderstood
☐ Feel angry
☐ Feel like crying
☐ Feel lonely
☐ Feel tired
☐ Feel sad
☐ Feel neutral
☐ Am taking it minute by minute

Date: /   /

If I need emotional support today, I will call:

____

My plans for today are: _______________________

____

____

My first thoughts of today: ___________________

____

My employer can help me during this time by:

____

I could use this from my spouse/significant other: _______________________

____

I'm really missing this about you... ___________________________________

____

Sometimes it feels like everyone has moved on, and I'm the only one that remembers you; that makes me...

____

____

I smiled when I remembered this about you... _____________________________

____

____

I find it helpful when: ____

____

I am comforted by: ____

____

I feel your presence most when... _______________________________________

____

If I can describe my day in one word, that word is: ______________________

Date: / /

If I need emotional support today, I will call:

____

My plans for today are: _________________________________

____

____

My first thoughts of today: ______________________________

____

My employer can help me during this time by:

____

I could use this from my spouse/significant other: _______________________

____

I'm really missing this about you... ___________________________________

____

Sometimes it feels like everyone has moved on, and I'm the only one that remembers you; that makes me...

____

____

I smiled when I remembered this about you... _________________________

____

____

I find it helpful when: ____

____

I am comforted by: ____

____

I feel your presence most when... ___________________________________

____

If I can describe my day in one word, that word is: ____________________

<table>
<tr><td colspan="2">Today I:</td></tr>
<tr><td>☐</td><td>Feel supported</td></tr>
<tr><td>☐</td><td>Feel brokenhearted</td></tr>
<tr><td>☐</td><td>Feel misunderstood</td></tr>
<tr><td>☐</td><td>Feel angry</td></tr>
<tr><td>☐</td><td>Feel like crying</td></tr>
<tr><td>☐</td><td>Feel lonely</td></tr>
<tr><td>☐</td><td>Feel tired</td></tr>
<tr><td>☐</td><td>Feel sad</td></tr>
<tr><td>☐</td><td>Feel neutral</td></tr>
<tr><td>☐</td><td>Am taking it minute by minute</td></tr>
</table>

$\mathcal{D}$ate: / /

If I need emotional support today, I will call:

____

My plans for today are: ________________________________

____

____

My first thoughts of today: ____________________________

____

My employer can help me during this time by:

____

I could use this from my spouse/significant other: ____________________________

____

I'm really missing this about you... ________________________________

____

Sometimes it feels like everyone has moved on, and I'm the only one that remembers you; that makes me...

____

____

I smiled when I remembered this about you... ________________________________

____

____

I find it helpful when: ________________________________

____

I am comforted by: ____________________________________

____

I feel your presence most when... ______________________________

____

If I can describe my day in one word, that word is: ____________________________

Today I:

- ☐ Feel supported
- ☐ Feel brokenhearted
- ☐ Feel misunderstood
- ☐ Feel angry
- ☐ Feel like crying
- ☐ Feel lonely
- ☐ Feel tired
- ☐ Feel sad
- ☐ Feel neutral
- ☐ Am taking it minute by minute

Date: / /

If I need emotional support today, I will call:

____

My plans for today are: _______________________________

____

____

My first thoughts of today: _______________________________

____

My employer can help me during this time by:

____

I could use this from my spouse/significant other: _______________________________

____

I'm really missing this about you... _______________________________

____

Sometimes it feels like everyone has moved on, and I'm the only one that remembers you; that makes me...

____

____

I smiled when I remembered this about you... _______________________________

____

____

I find it helpful when: _______________________________

____

I am comforted by: _______________________________

____

I feel your presence most when... _______________________________

____

If I can describe my day in one word, that word is: _______________________________

$\mathcal{D}ate$: / /

If I need emotional support today, I will call:

____

My plans for today are: _______________________

____

____

My first thoughts of today: ___________________

____

My employer can help me during this time by:

____

I could use this from my spouse/significant other: ___________________________

____

I'm really missing this about you... ___________________________________

____

Sometimes it feels like everyone has moved on, and I'm the only one that remembers you; that makes me...

____

____

I smiled when I remembered this about you... _______________________________

____

____

I find it helpful when: _______________________________________

____

I am comforted by: ____

____

I feel your presence most when... _______________________________________

____

If I can describe my day in one word, that word is: _______________________

Today I:

☐ Feel supported
☐ Feel brokenhearted
☐ Feel misunderstood
☐ Feel angry
☐ Feel like crying
☐ Feel lonely
☐ Feel tired
☐ Feel sad
☐ Feel neutral
☐ Am taking it minute by minute

$\mathcal{Date}$:   /   /

If I need emotional support today, I will call:

____

My plans for today are: _______________________

____

____

My first thoughts of today: ___________________

____

My employer can help me during this time by:

____

I could use this from my spouse/significant other: ______________________________

____

I'm really missing this about you... ____

____

Sometimes it feels like everyone has moved on, and I'm the only one that remembers you; that makes me...

____

____

I smiled when I remembered this about you... ____________________________________

____

____

I find it helpful when: ____

____

I am comforted by: ____

____

I feel your presence most when... ____

____

If I can describe my day in one word, that word is: _____________________________

Date: /   /

If I need emotional support today, I will call:

____

My plans for today are: _______________________

____

____

My first thoughts of today: ____________________

____

My employer can help me during this time by:

____

I could use this from my spouse/significant other: _______________________

____

I'm really missing this about you... _______________________

____

Sometimes it feels like everyone has moved on, and I'm the only one that remembers you; that makes me...

____

____

I smiled when I remembered this about you... _______________________

____

____

I find it helpful when: _______________________

____

I am comforted by: _______________________

____

I feel your presence most when... _______________________

____

If I can describe my day in one word, that word is: _______________________

Date: /   /

If I need emotional support today, I will call:

____

My plans for today are: _________________________________

____

____

My first thoughts of today: _______________________________

____

My employer can help me during this time by:

<table>
<tr><td>Today I:</td></tr>
<tr><td>☐ Feel supported</td></tr>
<tr><td>☐ Feel brokenhearted</td></tr>
<tr><td>☐ Feel misunderstood</td></tr>
<tr><td>☐ Feel angry</td></tr>
<tr><td>☐ Feel like crying</td></tr>
<tr><td>☐ Feel lonely</td></tr>
<tr><td>☐ Feel tired</td></tr>
<tr><td>☐ Feel sad</td></tr>
<tr><td>☐ Feel neutral</td></tr>
<tr><td>☐ Am taking it minute by minute</td></tr>
</table>

____

I could use this from my spouse/significant other: _______________________________

____

I'm really missing this about you... ____

____

Sometimes it feels like everyone has moved on, and I'm the only one that remembers you; that makes me...

____

____

I smiled when I remembered this about you... ___________________________________

____

____

I find it helpful when: ____

____

I am comforted by: ____

____

I feel your presence most when... ____

____

If I can describe my day in one word, that word is: _______________________________

$\mathcal{D}$ate: /   /

If I need emotional support today, I will call:

____

My plans for today are: _________________________

____

____

My first thoughts of today: ______________________

____

My employer can help me during this time by:

<table>
<tr><td colspan="2">𝓣oday I:</td></tr>
<tr><td>☐</td><td>Feel supported</td></tr>
<tr><td>☐</td><td>Feel brokenhearted</td></tr>
<tr><td>☐</td><td>Feel misunderstood</td></tr>
<tr><td>☐</td><td>Feel angry</td></tr>
<tr><td>☐</td><td>Feel like crying</td></tr>
<tr><td>☐</td><td>Feel lonely</td></tr>
<tr><td>☐</td><td>Feel tired</td></tr>
<tr><td>☐</td><td>Feel sad</td></tr>
<tr><td>☐</td><td>Feel neutral</td></tr>
<tr><td>☐</td><td>Am taking it minute by minute</td></tr>
</table>

____

I could use this from my spouse/significant other: _________________________

____

I'm really missing this about you... _________________________

____

Sometimes it feels like everyone has moved on, and I'm the only one that remembers you; that makes me...

____

____

I smiled when I remembered this about you... _________________________

____

____

I find it helpful when: _________________________

____

I am comforted by: _________________________

____

I feel your presence most when... _________________________

____

If I can describe my day in one word, that word is: _________________________

Date: / /

If I need emotional support today, I will call:

____

My plans for today are: _______________________

____

____

My first thoughts of today: ____________________

____

My employer can help me during this time by:

____

I could use this from my spouse/significant other: _______________________

____

I'm really missing this about you... _______________________

____

Sometimes it feels like everyone has moved on, and I'm the only one that remembers you; that makes me...

____

____

I smiled when I remembered this about you... _______________________

____

____

I find it helpful when: _______________________

____

I am comforted by: _______________________

____

I feel your presence most when... _______________________

____

If I can describe my day in one word, that word is: _______________________

<table>
<tr><td>Today I:</td></tr>
<tr><td>☐ Feel supported</td></tr>
<tr><td>☐ Feel brokenhearted</td></tr>
<tr><td>☐ Feel misunderstood</td></tr>
<tr><td>☐ Feel angry</td></tr>
<tr><td>☐ Feel like crying</td></tr>
<tr><td>☐ Feel lonely</td></tr>
<tr><td>☐ Feel tired</td></tr>
<tr><td>☐ Feel sad</td></tr>
<tr><td>☐ Feel neutral</td></tr>
<tr><td>☐ Am taking it minute by minute</td></tr>
</table>

$\mathcal{D}ate$:   /   /

If I need emotional support today, I will call:

____

My plans for today are: ______________________________

____

____

My first thoughts of today: ___________________________

____

My employer can help me during this time by:

____

I could use this from my spouse/significant other: ________________________

____

I'm really missing this about you... ______________________________________

____

Sometimes it feels like everyone has moved on, and I'm the only one that remembers you; that makes me...

____

____

I smiled when I remembered this about you... ____________________________

____

____

I find it helpful when: ____

____

I am comforted by: ____

____

I feel your presence most when... ______________________________________

____

If I can describe my day in one word, that word is: _______________________

<table>
<tr><td>

Today I:

☐ Feel supported
☐ Feel brokenhearted
☐ Feel misunderstood
☐ Feel angry
☐ Feel like crying
☐ Feel lonely
☐ Feel tired
☐ Feel sad
☐ Feel neutral
☐ Am taking it minute by minute

</td></tr>
</table>

Date: ___ / ___ / ___

If I need emotional support today, I will call:

____

My plans for today are: _______________________

____

____

My first thoughts of today: ___________________

____

My employer can help me during this time by:

____

I could use this from my spouse/significant other: _______________________________________

____

I'm really missing this about you... ____

____

Sometimes it feels like everyone has moved on, and I'm the only one that remembers you; that makes me...

____

____

I smiled when I remembered this about you... ____

____

____

I find it helpful when: ____

____

I am comforted by: ____

____

I feel your presence most when... ____

____

If I can describe my day in one word, that word is: _____________________________________

Date: /   /

If I need emotional support today, I will call:

____

My plans for today are: _________________________

____

____

My first thoughts of today: ______________________

____

My employer can help me during this time by:

____

I could use this from my spouse/significant other: _______________________________

____

I'm really missing this about you... ______________________________________

____

Sometimes it feels like everyone has moved on, and I'm the only one that remembers you; that makes me...

____

____

I smiled when I remembered this about you... _______________________________

____

____

I find it helpful when: ____

____

I am comforted by: ____

____

I feel your presence most when... ____

____

If I can describe my day in one word, that word is: _________________________

If I need emotional support today, I will call:

____

My plans for today are: _________________________

____

____

My first thoughts of today: ______________________

____

My employer can help me during this time by:

____

I could use this from my spouse/significant other: _______________________________

____

I'm really missing this about you... ______________________________________

____

Sometimes it feels like everyone has moved on, and I'm the only one that remembers you; that makes me...

____

____

I smiled when I remembered this about you... __________________________________

____

____

I find it helpful when: ____

____

I am comforted by: ____

____

I feel your presence most when... ____________________________________

____

If I can describe my day in one word, that word is: __________________________

Today I:

- ☐ Feel supported
- ☐ Feel brokenhearted
- ☐ Feel misunderstood
- ☐ Feel angry
- ☐ Feel like crying
- ☐ Feel lonely
- ☐ Feel tired
- ☐ Feel sad
- ☐ Feel neutral
- ☐ Am taking it minute by minute

Date: /   /

If I need emotional support today, I will call:

____

My plans for today are: _______________________________

____

____

My first thoughts of today: ____________________________

____

My employer can help me during this time by:

____

I could use this from my spouse/significant other: _______________________

____

I'm really missing this about you... _______________________________

____

Sometimes it feels like everyone has moved on, and I'm the only one that remembers you; that makes me...

____

____

I smiled when I remembered this about you... _______________________________

____

____

I find it helpful when: ________________________________

____

I am comforted by: ___________________________________

____

I feel your presence most when... ________________________

____

If I can describe my day in one word, that word is: _______________________

Today I:

☐ Feel supported
☐ Feel brokenhearted
☐ Feel misunderstood
☐ Feel angry
☐ Feel like crying
☐ Feel lonely
☐ Feel tired
☐ Feel sad
☐ Feel neutral
☐ Am taking it minute by minute

$\mathcal{Date:}$ /   /

If I need emotional support today, I will call:

____

My plans for today are: _______________________

____

____

My first thoughts of today: ____________________

____

My employer can help me during this time by:

____

I could use this from my spouse/significant other: ______________________

____

I'm really missing this about you... ____________________________________

____

Sometimes it feels like everyone has moved on, and I'm the only one that remembers you; that makes me...

____

____

I smiled when I remembered this about you... ____________________________

____

____

I find it helpful when: ____

____

I am comforted by: ____

____

I feel your presence most when... _______________________________________

____

If I can describe my day in one word, that word is: ______________________

Date: / /

If I need emotional support today, I will call:

____

My plans for today are: _______________________

____

____

My first thoughts of today: ____________________

____

My employer can help me during this time by:

____

I could use this from my spouse/significant other: _______________________

____

I'm really missing this about you... _______________________

____

Sometimes it feels like everyone has moved on, and I'm the only one that remembers you; that makes me...

____

____

I smiled when I remembered this about you... _______________________

____

____

I find it helpful when: _______________________

____

I am comforted by: _______________________

____

I feel your presence most when... _______________________

____

If I can describe my day in one word, that word is: _______________________

<table>
<tr><td>Today I:</td></tr>
<tr><td>☐ Feel supported</td></tr>
<tr><td>☐ Feel brokenhearted</td></tr>
<tr><td>☐ Feel misunderstood</td></tr>
<tr><td>☐ Feel angry</td></tr>
<tr><td>☐ Feel like crying</td></tr>
<tr><td>☐ Feel lonely</td></tr>
<tr><td>☐ Feel tired</td></tr>
<tr><td>☐ Feel sad</td></tr>
<tr><td>☐ Feel neutral</td></tr>
<tr><td>☐ Am taking it minute by minute</td></tr>
</table>

Date: /   /

If I need emotional support today, I will call:

____

My plans for today are: _______________________

____

____

My first thoughts of today: ____________________

____

My employer can help me during this time by:

____

I could use this from my spouse/significant other: ______________________________

____

I'm really missing this about you... ___________________________________

____

Sometimes it feels like everyone has moved on, and I'm the only one that remembers you; that makes me...

____

____

I smiled when I remembered this about you... ___________________________

____

____

I find it helpful when: ____

____

I am comforted by: ____

____

I feel your presence most when... _____________________________________

____

If I can describe my day in one word, that word is: ____________________

Today I:

☐ Feel supported
☐ Feel brokenhearted
☐ Feel misunderstood
☐ Feel angry
☐ Feel like crying
☐ Feel lonely
☐ Feel tired
☐ Feel sad
☐ Feel neutral
☐ Am taking it minute by minute

$\mathcal{Date:}$ /   /

If I need emotional support today, I will call:

____

My plans for today are: _______________________________

____

____

My first thoughts of today: _____________________________

____

My employer can help me during this time by:

$\mathcal{Today\ I:}$

☐ Feel supported

☐ Feel brokenhearted

☐ Feel misunderstood

☐ Feel angry

☐ Feel like crying

☐ Feel lonely

☐ Feel tired

☐ Feel sad

☐ Feel neutral

☐ Am taking it minute by minute

____

I could use this from my spouse/significant other: ___________________________

____

I'm really missing this about you... _________________________________

____

Sometimes it feels like everyone has moved on, and I'm the only one that remembers you; that makes me...

____

____

I smiled when I remembered this about you... ____________________________

____

____

I find it helpful when: _________________________________

____

I am comforted by: ___________________________________

____

I feel your presence most when... ______________________________

____

If I can describe my day in one word, that word is: ___________________

$\mathcal{D}ate$:   /   /

If I need emotional support today, I will call:

____

My plans for today are: _______________________

____

____

My first thoughts of today: ___________________

____

My employer can help me during this time by:

____

I could use this from my spouse/significant other: _______________________

____

I'm really missing this about you... _______________________

____

Sometimes it feels like everyone has moved on, and I'm the only one that remembers you; that makes me...

____

____

I smiled when I remembered this about you... _______________________

____

____

I find it helpful when: _______________________

____

I am comforted by: _______________________

____

I feel your presence most when... _______________________

____

If I can describe my day in one word, that word is: _______________________

Date: /   /

If I need emotional support today, I will call:

____

My plans for today are: _______________________

____

____

My first thoughts of today: ____________________

____

My employer can help me during this time by:

____

I could use this from my spouse/significant other: _______________________

____

I'm really missing this about you... _______________________________

____

Sometimes it feels like everyone has moved on, and I'm the only one that remembers you; that makes me...

____

____

I smiled when I remembered this about you... ____________________________

____

____

I find it helpful when: ____

____

I am comforted by: ____

____

I feel your presence most when... _______________________________

____

If I can describe my day in one word, that word is: _________________

<table>
<tr><td>Today I:</td></tr>
<tr><td>☐ Feel supported</td></tr>
<tr><td>☐ Feel brokenhearted</td></tr>
<tr><td>☐ Feel misunderstood</td></tr>
<tr><td>☐ Feel angry</td></tr>
<tr><td>☐ Feel like crying</td></tr>
<tr><td>☐ Feel lonely</td></tr>
<tr><td>☐ Feel tired</td></tr>
<tr><td>☐ Feel sad</td></tr>
<tr><td>☐ Feel neutral</td></tr>
<tr><td>☐ Am taking it minute by minute</td></tr>
</table>

Date: ___ / ___ / ___

If I need emotional support today, I will call:

____

My plans for today are: _______________________________

____

____

My first thoughts of today: ____________________________

____

My employer can help me during this time by:

____

I could use this from my spouse/significant other: ______________________

____

I'm really missing this about you... ____________________________________

____

Sometimes it feels like everyone has moved on, and I'm the only one that remembers you; that makes me...

____

____

I smiled when I remembered this about you... ____________________________

____

____

I find it helpful when: ____

____

I am comforted by: ____

____

I feel your presence most when... _______________________________________

____

If I can describe my day in one word, that word is: _____________________

Today I:

- ☐ Feel supported
- ☐ Feel brokenhearted
- ☐ Feel misunderstood
- ☐ Feel angry
- ☐ Feel like crying
- ☐ Feel lonely
- ☐ Feel tired
- ☐ Feel sad
- ☐ Feel neutral
- ☐ Am taking it minute by minute

Date: _____ / _____ / _____

If I need emotional support today, I will call:

____

My plans for today are: _______________________

____

____

My first thoughts of today: ___________________

____

My employer can help me during this time by:

____

I could use this from my spouse/significant other: _______________________

____

I'm really missing this about you... ___________________________________

____

Sometimes it feels like everyone has moved on, and I'm the only one that remembers you; that makes me...

____

____

I smiled when I remembered this about you... _______________________

____

____

I find it helpful when: ____

____

I am comforted by: ____

____

I feel your presence most when... _______________________________________

____

If I can describe my day in one word, that word is: _______________________

Today I:

☐ Feel supported
☐ Feel brokenhearted
☐ Feel misunderstood
☐ Feel angry
☐ Feel like crying
☐ Feel lonely
☐ Feel tired
☐ Feel sad
☐ Feel neutral
☐ Am taking it minute by minute

Date: / /

If I need emotional support today, I will call:

____

My plans for today are: _______________________________

____

____

My first thoughts of today: _____________________________

____

My employer can help me during this time by:

____

I could use this from my spouse/significant other: _____________________________

____

I'm really missing this about you... _________________________________

____

Sometimes it feels like everyone has moved on, and I'm the only one that remembers you; that makes me...

____

____

I smiled when I remembered this about you... _____________________________

____

____

I find it helpful when: _________________________________

____

I am comforted by: ___________________________________

____

I feel your presence most when... _______________________________

____

If I can describe my day in one word, that word is: _____________________

Date: /   /

If I need emotional support today, I will call:

____

My plans for today are: _______________________

____

____

My first thoughts of today: ___________________

____

My employer can help me during this time by:

____

I could use this from my spouse/significant other: _______________________________

____

I'm really missing this about you... _______________________________________

____

Sometimes it feels like everyone has moved on, and I'm the only one that remembers you; that makes me...

____

____

I smiled when I remembered this about you... _______________________________

____

____

I find it helpful when: ____

____

I am comforted by: ____

____

I feel your presence most when... _______________________________________

____

If I can describe my day in one word, that word is: _______________________

Date: / /

If I need emotional support today, I will call:

____

My plans for today are: _______________________

____

____

My first thoughts of today: ___________________

____

My employer can help me during this time by:

____

I could use this from my spouse/significant other: _______________________________________

____

I'm really missing this about you... ____

____

Sometimes it feels like everyone has moved on, and I'm the only one that remembers you; that makes me...

____

____

I smiled when I remembered this about you... _______________________________________

____

____

I find it helpful when: ____

____

I am comforted by: ____

____

I feel your presence most when... ____

____

If I can describe my day in one word, that word is: ___________________________________

Today I:

☐ Feel supported
☐ Feel brokenhearted
☐ Feel misunderstood
☐ Feel angry
☐ Feel like crying
☐ Feel lonely
☐ Feel tired
☐ Feel sad
☐ Feel neutral
☐ Am taking it minute by minute

Date: ___ / ___ / ___

If I need emotional support today, I will call:

____

My plans for today are: _______________________________

____

____

My first thoughts of today: ___________________________

____

My employer can help me during this time by:

____

I could use this from my spouse/significant other: ___________________________

____

I'm really missing this about you... _______________________________

____

Sometimes it feels like everyone has moved on, and I'm the only one that remembers you; that makes me...

____

____

I smiled when I remembered this about you... _______________________________

____

____

I find it helpful when: _______________________________

____

I am comforted by: _______________________________

____

I feel your presence most when... _______________________________

____

If I can describe my day in one word, that word is: _______________________

Date: ___ / ___ / ___

If I need emotional support today, I will call:

____

My plans for today are: _______________________

____

____

My first thoughts of today: ___________________

____

My employer can help me during this time by:

____

I could use this from my spouse/significant other: _______________________________________

____

I'm really missing this about you... ____

____

Sometimes it feels like everyone has moved on, and I'm the only one that remembers you; that makes me...

____

____

I smiled when I remembered this about you... ____

____

____

I find it helpful when: ____

____

I am comforted by: ____

____

I feel your presence most when... ____

____

If I can describe my day in one word, that word is: _______________________________________

Today I:
- ☐ Feel supported
- ☐ Feel brokenhearted
- ☐ Feel misunderstood
- ☐ Feel angry
- ☐ Feel like crying
- ☐ Feel lonely
- ☐ Feel tired
- ☐ Feel sad
- ☐ Feel neutral
- ☐ Am taking it minute by minute

Date: /   /

If I need emotional support today, I will call:

____

My plans for today are: _________________________________

____

____

My first thoughts of today: ______________________________

____

My employer can help me during this time by:

____

I could use this from my spouse/significant other: _____________________

____

I'm really missing this about you... ________________________________

____

Sometimes it feels like everyone has moved on, and I'm the only one that remembers you; that makes me...

____

____

I smiled when I remembered this about you... _____________________

____

____

I find it helpful when: ___________________________________

____

I am comforted by: _____________________________________

____

I feel your presence most when... _________________________

____

If I can describe my day in one word, that word is: ___________________

Date: /   /

If I need emotional support today, I will call:

____

My plans for today are: ___________________________________

____

____

My first thoughts of today: _________________________________

____

My employer can help me during this time by:

____

I could use this from my spouse/significant other: ___________________________________

____

I'm really missing this about you... ____

____

Sometimes it feels like everyone has moved on, and I'm the only one that remembers you; that makes me...

____

____

I smiled when I remembered this about you... __________________________________

____

____

I find it helpful when: ____

____

I am comforted by: ____

____

I feel your presence most when... ____

____

If I can describe my day in one word, that word is: _______________________________

<table>
<tr><td>Today I:</td></tr>
<tr><td>☐ Feel supported</td></tr>
<tr><td>☐ Feel brokenhearted</td></tr>
<tr><td>☐ Feel misunderstood</td></tr>
<tr><td>☐ Feel angry</td></tr>
<tr><td>☐ Feel like crying</td></tr>
<tr><td>☐ Feel lonely</td></tr>
<tr><td>☐ Feel tired</td></tr>
<tr><td>☐ Feel sad</td></tr>
<tr><td>☐ Feel neutral</td></tr>
<tr><td>☐ Am taking it minute by minute</td></tr>
</table>

Date: / /

If I need emotional support today, I will call:

____

My plans for today are: _________________________________

____

____

My first thoughts of today: ______________________________

____

My employer can help me during this time by:

____

I could use this from my spouse/significant other: __________________________

____

I'm really missing this about you... _______________________________________

____

Sometimes it feels like everyone has moved on, and I'm the only one that remembers you; that makes me...

____

____

I smiled when I remembered this about you... _______________________________

____

____

I find it helpful when: ____

____

I am comforted by: ____

____

I feel your presence most when... ____

____

If I can describe my day in one word, that word is: __________________________

<table>
<tr><td>Today I:</td></tr>
<tr><td>☐ Feel supported</td></tr>
<tr><td>☐ Feel brokenhearted</td></tr>
<tr><td>☐ Feel misunderstood</td></tr>
<tr><td>☐ Feel angry</td></tr>
<tr><td>☐ Feel like crying</td></tr>
<tr><td>☐ Feel lonely</td></tr>
<tr><td>☐ Feel tired</td></tr>
<tr><td>☐ Feel sad</td></tr>
<tr><td>☐ Feel neutral</td></tr>
<tr><td>☐ Am taking it minute by minute</td></tr>
</table>

Date: /   /

If I need emotional support today, I will call:

____

My plans for today are: _______________________________

____

____

My first thoughts of today: _______________________________

____

My employer can help me during this time by:

____

I could use this from my spouse/significant other: _______________________________

____

I'm really missing this about you... _______________________________

____

Sometimes it feels like everyone has moved on, and I'm the only one that remembers you; that makes me...

____

____

I smiled when I remembered this about you... _______________________________

____

____

I find it helpful when: _______________________________

____

I am comforted by: _______________________________

____

I feel your presence most when... _______________________________

____

If I can describe my day in one word, that word is: _______________________________

Today I:

☐ Feel supported
☐ Feel brokenhearted
☐ Feel misunderstood
☐ Feel angry
☐ Feel like crying
☐ Feel lonely
☐ Feel tired
☐ Feel sad
☐ Feel neutral
☐ Am taking it minute by minute

Date: /   /

If I need emotional support today, I will call:

____

My plans for today are: _______________________

____

____

My first thoughts of today: ____________________

____

My employer can help me during this time by:

____

I could use this from my spouse/significant other: ______________________________

____

I'm really missing this about you... ____

____

Sometimes it feels like everyone has moved on, and I'm the only one that remembers you; that makes me...

____

____

I smiled when I remembered this about you... __________________________________

____

____

I find it helpful when: ____

____

I am comforted by: ____

____

I feel your presence most when... ____

____

If I can describe my day in one word, that word is: ____________________________

Date: ___ / ___ / ___

If I need emotional support today, I will call:

____

My plans for today are: _______________________________

____

____

My first thoughts of today: _____________________________

____

My employer can help me during this time by:

____

I could use this from my spouse/significant other: _____________________

____

I'm really missing this about you... ________________________________

____

Sometimes it feels like everyone has moved on, and I'm the only one that remembers you; that makes me...

____

____

I smiled when I remembered this about you... ________________________

____

____

I find it helpful when: ________________________________

____

I am comforted by: ___________________________________

____

I feel your presence most when... _______________________________

____

If I can describe my day in one word, that word is: __________________

Today I:
- ☐ Feel supported
- ☐ Feel brokenhearted
- ☐ Feel misunderstood
- ☐ Feel angry
- ☐ Feel like crying
- ☐ Feel lonely
- ☐ Feel tired
- ☐ Feel sad
- ☐ Feel neutral
- ☐ Am taking it minute by minute

Date: / /

If I need emotional support today, I will call:

____

My plans for today are: _________________________

____

____

My first thoughts of today: _____________________

____

My employer can help me during this time by:

____

I could use this from my spouse/significant other: _________________________________

____

I'm really missing this about you... ____

____

Sometimes it feels like everyone has moved on, and I'm the only one that remembers you; that makes me...

____

____

I smiled when I remembered this about you... _______________________________

____

____

I find it helpful when: ____

____

I am comforted by: ____

____

I feel your presence most when... _______________________________________

____

If I can describe my day in one word, that word is: _______________________

Date: / /

If I need emotional support today, I will call:

____

My plans for today are: _________________________

____

____

My first thoughts of today: ______________________

____

My employer can help me during this time by:

____

I could use this from my spouse/significant other: _______________________________

____

I'm really missing this about you... ____

____

Sometimes it feels like everyone has moved on, and I'm the only one that remembers you; that makes me...

____

____

I smiled when I remembered this about you... ____________________________________

____

____

I find it helpful when: ____

____

I am comforted by: ____

____

I feel your presence most when... ____

____

If I can describe my day in one word, that word is: ______________________________

Date: /   /

If I need emotional support today, I will call:

____

My plans for today are: _______________________

____

____

My first thoughts of today: ____________________

____

My employer can help me during this time by:

____

I could use this from my spouse/significant other: ___________________________

____

I'm really missing this about you... ____

____

Sometimes it feels like everyone has moved on, and I'm the only one that remembers you; that makes me...

____

____

I smiled when I remembered this about you... _______________________________

____

____

I find it helpful when: ____

____

I am comforted by: ____

____

I feel your presence most when... ____

____

If I can describe my day in one word, that word is: _________________________

Today I:

☐ Feel supported
☐ Feel brokenhearted
☐ Feel misunderstood
☐ Feel angry
☐ Feel like crying
☐ Feel lonely
☐ Feel tired
☐ Feel sad
☐ Feel neutral
☐ Am taking it minute by minute

$Date$: / /

If I need emotional support today, I will call:

____

My plans for today are: _______________________

____

____

My first thoughts of today: ___________________

____

My employer can help me during this time by:

Today I:

☐ Feel supported
☐ Feel brokenhearted
☐ Feel misunderstood
☐ Feel angry
☐ Feel like crying
☐ Feel lonely
☐ Feel tired
☐ Feel sad
☐ Feel neutral
☐ Am taking it minute by minute

____

I could use this from my spouse/significant other: ___________________________

____

I'm really missing this about you... ____

____

Sometimes it feels like everyone has moved on, and I'm the only one that remembers you; that makes me...

____

____

I smiled when I remembered this about you... _________________________________

____

____

I find it helpful when: ____

____

I am comforted by: ____

____

I feel your presence most when... ____

____

If I can describe my day in one word, that word is: ___________________________

Date: /   /

If I need emotional support today, I will call:

____

My plans for today are: _______________________

____

____

My first thoughts of today: ___________________

____

My employer can help me during this time by:

____

I could use this from my spouse/significant other: _______________________

____

I'm really missing this about you... _______________________

____

Sometimes it feels like everyone has moved on, and I'm the only one that remembers you; that makes me...

____

____

I smiled when I remembered this about you... _______________________

____

____

I find it helpful when: _______________________

____

I am comforted by: _______________________

____

I feel your presence most when... _______________________

____

If I can describe my day in one word, that word is: _______________________

Date: /   /

If I need emotional support today, I will call:

____

My plans for today are: _______________________________

____

____

My first thoughts of today: ____________________________

____

My employer can help me during this time by:

____

I could use this from my spouse/significant other: _______________________________

____

I'm really missing this about you... ____

____

Sometimes it feels like everyone has moved on, and I'm the only one that remembers you; that makes me...

____

____

I smiled when I remembered this about you... _______________________________

____

____

I find it helpful when: ____

____

I am comforted by: ____

____

I feel your presence most when... ____

____

If I can describe my day in one word, that word is: ___________________________

Today I:

☐ Feel supported
☐ Feel brokenhearted
☐ Feel misunderstood
☐ Feel angry
☐ Feel like crying
☐ Feel lonely
☐ Feel tired
☐ Feel sad
☐ Feel neutral
☐ Am taking it minute by minute

Date: /   /

If I need emotional support today, I will call:

____

My plans for today are: ______________________

____

____

My first thoughts of today: __________________

____

My employer can help me during this time by:

____

I could use this from my spouse/significant other: ___________________________

____

I'm really missing this about you... ___________________________________

____

Sometimes it feels like everyone has moved on, and I'm the only one that remembers you; that makes me...

____

____

I smiled when I remembered this about you... ____________________________

____

____

I find it helpful when: ____

____

I am comforted by: ____

____

I feel your presence most when... _______________________________

____

If I can describe my day in one word, that word is: _______________________

Date: ___ / ___ / ___

If I need emotional support today, I will call:

____

My plans for today are: _________________________

____

____

My first thoughts of today: _____________________

____

My employer can help me during this time by:

____

I could use this from my spouse/significant other: _______________________________

____

I'm really missing this about you... _______________________________________

____

Sometimes it feels like everyone has moved on, and I'm the only one that remembers you; that makes me...

____

____

I smiled when I remembered this about you... _______________________________

____

____

I find it helpful when: ____

____

I am comforted by: ____

____

I feel your presence most when... ____

____

If I can describe my day in one word, that word is: _______________________

Today I:

☐ Feel supported
☐ Feel brokenhearted
☐ Feel misunderstood
☐ Feel angry
☐ Feel like crying
☐ Feel lonely
☐ Feel tired
☐ Feel sad
☐ Feel neutral
☐ Am taking it minute by minute

Date: / /

If I need emotional support today, I will call:

____

My plans for today are: _______________________

____

____

My first thoughts of today: ____________________

____

My employer can help me during this time by:

____

I could use this from my spouse/significant other: _______________________________

____

I'm really missing this about you... _______________________________________

____

Sometimes it feels like everyone has moved on, and I'm the only one that remembers you; that makes me...

____

____

I smiled when I remembered this about you... ______________________________

____

____

I find it helpful when: ____

____

I am comforted by: ____

____

I feel your presence most when... ______________________________________

____

If I can describe my day in one word, that word is: ____________________

Date: /   /

If I need emotional support today, I will call:

____

My plans for today are: _______________________________

____

____

My first thoughts of today: ____________________________

____

My employer can help me during this time by:

____

I could use this from my spouse/significant other: ________________________________

____

I'm really missing this about you... ____

____

Sometimes it feels like everyone has moved on, and I'm the only one that remembers you; that makes me...

____

____

I smiled when I remembered this about you... ____________________________________

____

____

I find it helpful when: ____

____

I am comforted by: ____

____

I feel your presence most when... ____

____

If I can describe my day in one word, that word is: ________________________________

Today I:
☐ Feel supported
☐ Feel brokenhearted
☐ Feel misunderstood
☐ Feel angry
☐ Feel like crying
☐ Feel lonely
☐ Feel tired
☐ Feel sad
☐ Feel neutral
☐ Am taking it minute by minute

Date: /   /

If I need emotional support today, I will call:

____

My plans for today are: _________________________

____

____

My first thoughts of today: ______________________

____

My employer can help me during this time by:

____

I could use this from my spouse/significant other: _______________________________

____

I'm really missing this about you... _______________________________________

____

Sometimes it feels like everyone has moved on, and I'm the only one that remembers you; that makes me...

____

____

I smiled when I remembered this about you... _______________________________

____

____

I find it helpful when: ____

____

I am comforted by: ____

____

I feel your presence most when... ____

____

If I can describe my day in one word, that word is: _______________________________

<table>
<tr><th>Today I:</th></tr>
<tr><td>☐ Feel supported</td></tr>
<tr><td>☐ Feel brokenhearted</td></tr>
<tr><td>☐ Feel misunderstood</td></tr>
<tr><td>☐ Feel angry</td></tr>
<tr><td>☐ Feel like crying</td></tr>
<tr><td>☐ Feel lonely</td></tr>
<tr><td>☐ Feel tired</td></tr>
<tr><td>☐ Feel sad</td></tr>
<tr><td>☐ Feel neutral</td></tr>
<tr><td>☐ Am taking it minute by minute</td></tr>
</table>

Date: /   /

If I need emotional support today, I will call:

____

My plans for today are: _______________________________

____

____

My first thoughts of today: _____________________________

____

My employer can help me during this time by:

____

I could use this from my spouse/significant other: ___________________________________

____

I'm really missing this about you... ____

____

Sometimes it feels like everyone has moved on, and I'm the only one that remembers you; that makes me...

____

____

I smiled when I remembered this about you... _________________________________

____

____

I find it helpful when: ____

____

I am comforted by: ____

____

I feel your presence most when... ____

____

If I can describe my day in one word, that word is: _______________________________

Today I:

☐ Feel supported

☐ Feel brokenhearted

☐ Feel misunderstood

☐ Feel angry

☐ Feel like crying

☐ Feel lonely

☐ Feel tired

☐ Feel sad

☐ Feel neutral

☐ Am taking it minute by minute

Date: / /

If I need emotional support today, I will call:

____

My plans for today are: _______________________

____

____

My first thoughts of today: ____________________

____

My employer can help me during this time by:

____

I could use this from my spouse/significant other: _______________________

____

I'm really missing this about you... _______________________

____

Sometimes it feels like everyone has moved on, and I'm the only one that remembers you; that makes me...

____

____

I smiled when I remembered this about you... _______________________

____

____

I find it helpful when: _______________________

____

I am comforted by: _______________________

____

I feel your presence most when... _______________________

____

If I can describe my day in one word, that word is: _______________________

Today I:

☐ Feel supported
☐ Feel brokenhearted
☐ Feel misunderstood
☐ Feel angry
☐ Feel like crying
☐ Feel lonely
☐ Feel tired
☐ Feel sad
☐ Feel neutral
☐ Am taking it minute by minute

$\mathcal{D}ate$:   /   /

If I need emotional support today, I will call:

____

My plans for today are: _______________________________

____

____

My first thoughts of today: _____________________________

____

My employer can help me during this time by:

____

I could use this from my spouse/significant other: _____________________________

____

I'm really missing this about you... _________________________________

____

Sometimes it feels like everyone has moved on, and I'm the only one that remembers you; that makes me...

____

____

I smiled when I remembered this about you... _________________________________

____

____

I find it helpful when: ____

____

I am comforted by: ____

____

I feel your presence most when... _________________________________

____

If I can describe my day in one word, that word is: _____________________________

I will honor your legacy by:

I will honor your legacy by:

1. Talk about your loved one daily
2. Write down your thoughts about your loved one as they occur to you
3. Record your dreams about your departed loved one
4. Wear their favorite color
5. Dine at their favorite restaurant on a special occasion
6. Memorialize and update their social media pages
7. Create a memorial website with pictures and space for reflections from loved ones and friends
8. Plant a memorial tree
9. Organize a balloon release on special occasions
10. Visit their final resting spot frequently
11. Stay in contact with your loved one's closest friends and exchange memories
12. Create photo pillows and blankets with their image
13. Complete things they wanted to complete but they did not complete (I wrote and released a published book because my mom always wanted to be a published author)
14. Create and maintain a garden of their favorite fruits or vegetables
15. Honor their spirit during special occasions by placing a single rose in a chair honoring their spiritual presence
16. Celebrate /Acknowledge their heavenly birthdays
17. Commit Random Acts of Kindness
18. Create or join social media groups & exchange memories with others who have lost loved ones
19. Burn their favorite scented candles
20. Create a sacred box that includes precious items of your loved one
21. Name your child after your loved one
22. Go on a vacation that your loved one always wanted to go on
23. Walk on the beach barefoot and allow beautiful memories to flow about your loved one

24. Donate to their favorite charity/organization
25. Ask their favorite employer to create and hang a memorial plaque
26. Commit to adding different color bouquets every month at their gravesite
27. Care for their pet or adopt a pet in their honor
28. Speak of your loved one unapologetically
29. Wear jewelry that reminds you of your loved one (I wear bee jewelry to feel close to my mom's spirit since I always called her Miss Bee)
30. Say good morning to your loved one's spirit when you wake and goodnight at night
31. Play their favorite music, and dance while thinking happy memories

List Additional Ways to Keep Your Loved One's Spirit Alive

____

____

____

____

____

____

____

____

____

There is no right or wrong way to honor your loved one's legacy or how to keep their spirit alive.

Whatever you do, don't abandon their spirit.

Kinyatta E. Gray is a motherless daughter, published author, and FlightsInStilettos Founder & CEO.

Website
https://www.flightsinstilettos.com/

Disclaimer: Kinyatta E. Gray is not a mental health provider and is providing this information based on real-life experience and to inspire others to keep their loved one's legacy alive. If you are experiencing a physical or emotional crisis, seek the help of a mental health professional.

OTHER GUIDED JOURNALS & DIARIES *by* KINYATTA E. GRAY

I Miss You...

Daily Writing Prompts for Reflection, Remembrance, and Spirit Renewal

The "Hallelujah" Notes

Sunday Worship Notes & Reflections

Fashionista's Travel Diary

A Guided Travel Diary for Travel Planning & Reflections

Caring for Every Inch of Me

Daily Reflections for Self-Care & Spirit Renewal

I'm Doing Me

The Ultimate Breakup Diary for Venting, Reflection & Spirit Renewal

Chapter 30

Capturing Life, Love & Lessons in my 30s

While I'm Still Here

A Guided Expression Journal of Life, Love and Legacy for Those Preparing to Transition

Chapter 40

Capturing Life, Love & Lessons in my 40s

My Crazy Teenage Life

The Ultimate Expression Diary for Venting, Self-Reflections and Self-Love

Chapter 50

Capturing Life, Love & Lessons in my 50s

I Am A Man. I Have Feelings.

A Guided 90-Day Self-Reflections & Gratitude Journal for Men

Chapter 60

Capturing Life, Love & Lessons in my 60s

The Queen's Manifestation Journal

Daily Writing Prompt for Manifesting the Life You Want

Sweet Sixteen

Capturing Life, Love & Lessons in my teens

Budget & Shop

A Monthly Personal Budget & Expense Tracker for Young Adults

Remembering Mom

A Grief Journal for Reflections and Remembrance

My Life My Love My Truth

LGBTQ journal

Men Have Feelings Too

A Guided 60-day. Self-Reflections, Self-Care & Gratitude Journal for Men

Sexy Baby Mama

Self-Love | Self-Reflections | Spirit Renewal

"I miss you. I love you. I'm learning to live without you. I'm taking it day by day for as long as it takes."

Kinyatta E. Gray

AUTHOR & CELEBRITY TRAVEL INFLUENCER